TEACHING READING

TO THE

DISADVANTAGED ADULT

Teaching Reading

to the

Disadvantaged Adult

by

Dr. James A. Dinnan

University of Georgia

Dr. Curtis Ulmer, *Editor*

University of Georgia

Prentice-Hall Adult Education Series

Prentice-Hall, Inc.   *Englewood Cliffs, N.J.*

PRINTED IN THE UNITED STATES OF AMERICA
ISBN—0-13-894048-7
ENCY

INTRODUCTION

It seems clear that lack of testing, reliance upon grade completion criteria, and inadequate definitions of functional literacy combine to produce serious official underestimates of the extent of illiteracy in the United States.[1]

This statement included three major areas used for identifying illiterates. They are those individuals who cannot function at the minimum level required for them in the work structure of an industrialized society. A complex technological society, where one doughnut machine put 600 men and women on the unemployment roles, requires an individual to be able to function at a level beyond that of pure manual labor. They must not only be able to orally communicate with a co-worker, or a social group, but be able to read and follow specific directions, print clearly enough so that others may follow their directions, and handle simple to complex mathematical problems. Everyday living requires these skills.

The person who tries to enter into the work-stream of a highly impersonal technological society without the fundamental tools of basic communication, reading, writing, and mathematics, is almost at a complete loss before he starts. Don Parker in his searching book, *Schooling for What?* [2] interviewed a thousand human beings involved in every aspect of our society and provides a broad spectrum of the needed revisions of schooling for today's society.

---

[1] David Harman, *Illiteracy: An Overview*. Harvard Educational Review, 1970, 40:2.
[2] Don H. Parker, *Schooling for What?* New York: McGraw-Hill, 1970.

Robinson [3] notes the adult teacher is faced with the dilemma of quickly ascertaining each student's current reading status without ridiculing him or inducing failure. This is extremely important to the ultimate success of the teaching program.

Ulmer states:

> The biggest disadvantages of being an adult student are those the student creates for himself: Anxieties and inferiority feelings about his ability to succeed in the classroom. The adult student who has been away from school for many years often has a very damaged picture of his academic capabilities. This is especially true of the adult who dropped out or was expelled from school. This student may be wracked with anxiety about his ability to succeed in an adventure which was disastrous once before or about his ability to return to the world of words and ideas. Unfortunately, his anxieties are reinforced by current myths about the learning abilities of adults, by unpleasant memories of multiplication tables and by the nagging belief that school is, after all, only for children. [4]

The Georgia prison director indicated that over 90% of the prison inmates had no salable skills to offer an employer other than their presence in the world. Most of these inmates were in very poor shape when it came to basic communication skills. They were not all mentally incompetent but were lacking the tools demanded in today's technological society. The social, emotional, or natural circumstances that produce or influence human actions must all enter into the consideration of each group or individual. The basic consideration presented in this text will be the human and his reaction to the world about him, how he learns, and how he can learn to handle the written symbol.

This manual has been designed to assess the background of the individual and to bring him to the stage of unlocking the symbolic codes we call Reading and Mathematics. The basic intellectual process is the same for *both* these codes, only the symbols are different. (Likewise art and music are different codes to be broken by an individual, but the process remains the *same* in all written codes presented to the intellect.)

JAMES A. DINNAN

---

[3] Richard Robinson, *An Investigation into the use of the Cloze Procedure with a Group of Functionally Illiterate Adults.* Unpublished Doctoral Dissertation, University of Georgia.

[4] Curtis Ulmer, *Teaching the Disadvantaged Adult.* Nat. Assoc. of Pub. School Adult Educators, 1969.

CONTENTS

INTRODUCTION **5**

INTRODUCTION TO A SYMBOLIC CODE **9**

    The Thinking Process **9**
    The Key to Learning Basis **11**

BASIC READING SKILLS **12**

    Readiness **12**
    Visual Discrimination **15**
    Auditory Discrimination **17**
    Writing Visual-Motor Coordination **21**
    Written Symbolic Code-Mathematics **26**

COMPREHENSION **28**

    Operations of the Intellect **28**
    Stimulus Content Through the Senses **29**
    Products (Internal) **30**
    Comprehension of the Reading Material **31**

ORGANIZING AN ADULT GROUP FOR INSTRUCTION **37**

    Possible Material for Adults **39**
    Physical Testing **39**

Selected Bibliography **43**

Contents

Appendix A **46**

    Positional References **46**
    Volume References **47**

Appendix B **48**

    Oral Language Exam **48**
    Oral Language Exam A **48**

INTRODUCTION TO A SYMBOLIC CODE

A symbolic code might be classified as an action or a sign that has been agreed upon by two or more people to represent something in their world.

"Profiles of sounds provided by newborn infants show no differences over racial, cultural, or language groups." [5] This statement indicates that language is acquired through contact with other humans who agree on a set of oral sounds or actions and use them to represent things in the world they live in. Thus we have a basic human organism being activated by stimulus progressing to a stage of language development. There is no difference, except in the capacity of the organism itself, or the condition of the input receivers, until the different stimulus is received, processed, and recorded by the individual. He then grows and is responsive to the world around him and develops a language and customs, to a large extent, of his total environment. German, English, Spanish, Hausa, and Chinese are all languages learned by processing the stimulus data through the intellect.

The language code is used to explain the actions of the environment about him, or other human actions. When the explanation of behavior, environment or human, is written into symbols there must again be agreement as to the meaning of these symbols. All the written codes have several things in common. First, they all use lines, music (𝄞), art (🏠), numbers (1,2,3) and reading (boy-girl). Second, they must represent something known to the readers if they are to have any meaning. Third, they are used to explain human or environmental action.

These actions have been classified into two separate categories, namely, the Arts (Human) and the Sciences (Environment). One is an explanation or presentation of human behavior and the other an explanation or presentation of the behavior of non-human matter.

The Thinking Process

In order for a person to understand the reading process it is necessary for him to review the process involved in thinking. Reading involves thinking at all levels, or stages of development.

When an external stimulus is presented to the intellect for processing, it is first received through the basic senses. Sight, hearing, taste, smell, or touch are the basic transmitters of information to the intellect. These might be considered as the input receivers.

If a person received a sound input, the vibrations are transmitted through the nerve fibers to the intellect for processing.

$$\text{sound} \rightarrow \text{intellect (process)} \rightarrow \text{output}$$

---

[5] Nelson Brooks, Language and Language Learning. New York: Harcourt, 1964.

The sight input receiver, or any of the other senses, would operate in the same manner.

$$sight \rightarrow intellect \ (process) \rightarrow output$$

These input receivers, the senses, are limited by their physical capacities and the amount of stimulus presented. For example, if a sound were beyond the level of vibration threshold of the human organism (a high pitch dog whistle) or not being able to see a micro-organism, hydrogen in air, or an atom with the naked eye, they would both result in no communication. The sensory impressions that are within the range of an individual's capacity are transmitted to the intellect for processing. This intellectual process takes place through *one* (external or internal) sensory input placed against *one* memory unit.

When a person hears a given sound, for instance a car horn, the intellect receives the stimulus and matches it with a previously stored memory unit and compares the *one input* unit to *one stored* memory unit and the results can either be stored in the memory or produce an external act shown by the person saying, "That's a car horn." The process of data by the intellect is *one* unit against *one* unit. It is extremely rapid in its operation and the more memory units brought into the process the more detailed the results. An example might be a dog bark:

$$bark \ input \rightarrow bark \ (memory \ unit) \rightarrow . \ Yes \ it \ is \ a \ \text{``bark.''}$$

Is it a big dog or a small dog? Is it a young dog or an old dog? Is the dog near or far? All of these memory units could be brought into the process (*one* at a time in rapid succession) to produce the statement "That is a big dog, far away."

The process of the intellect is *comparing* an input unit to a stored memory unit and producing another unit on the basis of comparing the two. The comparisons are made with either volume or positional references. Volume includes such comparisons as size, big-small, short-long, or number, none-two, one-five. Position includes such comparisons as on-off, front-back, open-closed, high-middle-low.

The "intellect" is using the relative position or volume of the unit presented for processing. We understand something only in relation to something else. For example, is this guide big or little? You can only answer that question in relation to some other printed guide. If the one you compare it with has 500 pages, this guide is little. If you compare it to a guide which has only 4 pages, this guide is big. The intellect processes information by *comparing* it with another piece of stored information.

The Key to Learning [6] Basis

The basis for reading, or any other symbolic code, is the common association of the sender and the receiver with the stimulus presented. If communication is the object of the transmission then both the sender and the receiver must have a common understanding of the act, otherwise no communication will take place. For example, if someone said to you, "Bu tie lay," what did he mean? Unless you understand Chinese you would not get the intended message. No communication would take place. You would know he spoke to you, but only that he said something, not understanding what he said. If there were 200 cars parked in a lot and someone gave you a key (nothing else) and said, "Would you bring the car to the lady?," you would request further information to help you select the right car, otherwise you must try each car until you find the one the key fits. (Please bring the red Pontiac parked in slot number three, in the last row, to the lady.)

Each time a reference is made to an object the intellectual process depends upon the ability of the individual to compare the stimulus words presented. Look at the data presented to the person finding the car.

red

Pontiac

parked

slot

three

last

row

All of these indicate its volume or its position and each must be compared with something else in order to understand the message sent by the speaker or writer. What do you do with it when you have located the car? *Bring to lady*. Again it is the position and volume references that must be compared to finally complete the requested act. Our whole language, written or spoken, is based upon a *common* understanding of items in terms of position and volume.

The following development of the teaching of reading to adults is based upon the "thinking process" and the need for a clear understanding of the necessary data a new reader must process in order to understand the communication of an author, or writer, in the initial and advanced stages of understanding a written code.

---

[6] James A. Dinnan. "The Key to Learning," *Journal of Reading Behavior*. Winter 1971, Vol. 3:1.

The basic associations of a student and a teacher must be the *same* if they are to learn to unlock the code. If both have different associations to stimulus, then *no* communication will take place.

BASIC READING SKILLS

Readiness

"Readiness" for reading a symbolic code has often been connected with young children. Preschool or kindergarten training where oral expression, physical actions within a group situation, seeing and identifying many common objects has surrounded this concept. Adults bring into the class situation a vastly broader concept of the world around them, because of the years of experience of everyday living, than do young children.

"Readiness" training has two major aspects. The first is the physical, emotional, social readiness for learning and the second is the mental development of an individual assuring proper use of associational tasks that will enable him to understand instruction involved in learning a written code. Adult readiness training should concentrate strongly upon the second aspect.

Learning a written code, such as the one we use in English, involves the twenty-six letters of the alphabet and the major sound connected with these written symbols. The combination of these written symbols and their sounds assist the students to unlock the 500,000 words used in our language. The object is not to learn a specific word like *man* or *car* but to enable them to generalize all of the possible combinations these twenty-six symbols and sounds might represent. In other words, to give them the key to unlock the code in all of its broad aspects.

Since these adults have mastered, to a great extent, a large portion of the oral language used in communicating with other individuals, the readiness training can begin by developing the necessary position and volume references they will need to understand the written symbol.

The introduction of this guide developed the idea that in order to observe an item it is necessary to understand a contrasting position or volume reference. All written codes use *lines* as the basis of their symbols. If a teacher were to explain these line symbols she must use basic references to the position, or volume, of the line or lines she is presenting. For example, this might be a teacher's explanation of the shape of the letter "b" and how to print it.

"This is the alphabet letter 'b.' You make a straight line from the top of the line to the bottom line like this, then you start a half circle at the back in the middle of the line like this, and bring it to the bottom of the straight line like this. This is how we make the letter 'b.' It is a high letter."

Let's examine the necessary mental references needed to understand what has been said by the teacher. Here are the positional words used:

> straight
> top
> bottom
> start
> circle
> middle
> back
> high

The volume words used in the instructions were:

> a (one)
> half

What might be considered by the teacher as a simple set of instructions is really a complex set of associations that a learner must have in order for him to understand this communication. The student can make this letter by simple rote production, but remember, he will be asked to generalize it in thousands of words, in many positions. If you ask him to repeat after you $a + b = c$, he can do it, but what does it mean?

You can only see one thing in relation to another thing, even if it has only been stored in the memory, and both of the things must be measured by the same association. When the teacher stated that "b" was a high letter, what was it high in relation to? In order to see a high letter, a middle or low letter must be presented at the same time such as "b-a, b-p."

The instructions indicated, back of the line, this concept includes that "left to right" is the *correct* front and back of a vertical line. Without this basic concept "front-back" has no definite position, it could be either way, as could be "start-finish."

Further analysis of these "simple" directions reveals that the common associations that the teacher is using, and assuming that the learner is also using, to explain a single letter are contrasted with the following:

> straight — curved
> top   — bottom
> start   — finish
> circle   — straight
> middle — top (bottom)
> one   — two (none)
> half   — whole

Readiness must be undertaken, with the adult learner, to assure complete agreement with the oral instruction given by a teacher as to the meanings associated with the position and volume of lines when teaching visual discrimination of the alphabet.

Many different concepts or associations are connected by a learner to a given stimulus word. Recently, several research projects have been directed towards identification of the various types of responses given by readers and non-readers. Bickley [7] noted that the types of oral associations made by the subjects could be used as a predictor of performance on tests which had a frame of reference that required a specific type of association, namely, contrast, whole-part, coordinate, superordinate relations. The subjects whose association to oral stimulus words were directly connected with personal experience, a closure, did significantly poorer on formalized tests.

Examples of closure using the positional and volume words presented in the sample lesson are these types of responses, associations, to stimulus words.

Stimulus Words		*Closure Type Responses*
straight	—	whiskey
top	—	draw
bottom	—	of the pile
start	—	motor
circle	—	traffic
middle	—	belly
back	—	home
high	—	drunk

Readiness then should be considered as preparing an individual to automatically associate the positional and volume references in terms of a contract. The major positional and volume references are presented in Appendix A. These references were selected from Fitzgerald's [8] basic communication vocabulary which presents a composite of the major words used, oral and written, in the English language. The important factor is not only that they can say or use a word but that they have a specific association to position and volume contrast when they use such words as on-off, front-back, high-low, open-closed, none-one, big-small, short-tall, loud-soft, or left-right. The teacher must have the student demonstrate his knowledge of these references by acting out, moving items to a specific position, picking up or pointing to, items as they appear in real life or pictures. The student must demonstrate *both* contrasting associations when performing the act or orally responding to the references.

---

[7] A. C. Bickley, J. A. Dinnan, and R. Bickley, Language associations as a predictor of performance on an intelligence test. *Journal of Reading Behavior*, 1970, 2, 291–294.

[8] James A. Fitzgerald and Patricia Fitzgerald. *Reading and the Language Arts*. Milwaukee: Bruce Pub., 1965.

The teacher must be careful in requesting these references. An example might be a picture of a large truck and a small car. If the instructor asks the person to point to the "large truck" and then to point to the "small car" the only key in this action is the truck or the car. Large or small have not necessarily been demonstrated. In order to demonstrate large-small, the *same item* should be used. Pointing to a large truck, a small truck, a large car, a small car is a far better question for observing large-small relationships.

The entire list (Appendix A) should be completely mastered, and automatically responded to, before any attempt is made to teach the students written symbols.

The oral examination presented in Appendix B can be used to check the predominant method of responding to oral stimuli by an individual before entering him into the written code.

Visual Discrimination

When any item is recognized as different from something else, some form of discrimination has taken place. The difference between a Ford car and a Volkswagen is apparent in its shape and size. A further investigation would reveal many more differences such as an air-cooled motor versus a water-cooled motor and so on. Visual discrimination of symbols used in a written code can be studied in the same manner, from large apparent differences to finer differences. An important concept to be recognized at this point is that no student should be put into the reading code until he has been assessed "ready" by demonstrating an automatic response to the positional and volume reference presented in Appendix A.

The basis for our written language code consists of lines made into twenty-six letters. However, it is not as simple as many educators think. If lines, and the shape of lines, form our written language and these lines only took one form, our task of teaching discrimination of letters would be made much simpler. The shape of the same letter found within a single classroom ranges anywhere from five to nine different shapes.

$$a \; a \; a \; a \; A \; A \; a \; A \; A$$

The first contact with the written symbols should be one in which large discrimination factors are apparent, once learned, then a further discrimination pattern may be introduced. The major portion of print used in English writing, newspapers, books, texts, or magazines is found in this type of standard lower/case print.

a b c d e f g h i j k l m n o p q r s t u v w x y z

The major discriminations of these letters are the high letters, middle letters, and low letters.

High Letters
b d f h k l t

Middle Letters
a c e i m n o r s u v w x z

Low Letters
g j p q y

The teacher should *print* the lower/case standard print on the board in proper sequence. Be sure you use the proper letters such as a, g, f, q, k when presenting the *standard* lower/case alphabet.

The first step should be to have the students observe the high, middle, low letters. They do not even, at this point, have to name the letter, but only to discriminate that it is a high, middle, or low letter.

The next step would be to *print* each lower/case *standard* letter on a separate card (half of a Manila folder) and have the students classify the letters by putting them into three groups: high, middle, and low letters. Remember, a person can only observe a high letter if it is placed *next to* a low or middle letter. When these letters are demonstrated by the students they must use two different types of letters, high-low, high-middle, middle-low, and so on.

The names of the letters should be introduced using its general configuration pattern as an additional identification of specific letters. Always introduce two different letters at a time.

This is the letter a; it is a middle letter.
This is the letter b; it is a high letter.

This is the letter n; it is a middle letter.
This is the letter y; it is a low letter.

This is the letter k; it is a high letter.
This is the letter p; it is a low letter.

As these standard lower/case letters are introduced by name, the writing (printing) section of this guide should be taught at the same time.

A further discrimination of these twenty-six letters will reveal finer discrimination points. Some examples are:

d the curved line is in front
b the curved line is in back

l is a tall letter
i is a short letter

o is a closed curved line
c is an open curved line

n has two straight lines (one space)
m has three straight lines (two spaces)

The final step in visual discrimination of the lower/case standard print letters might be the awareness of long and short words and how these words are made from a combination of high-middle-low letters. Print six or eight long and short words on the board. An example might be:

tie	water	elephant
together	he	big

Have the students identify the high, middle, and low letters in these words. Then have them decide which are the long words and which are the short words. At this point you might ask the students to give you several long and short words and print them on the board. A note of caution: since most teachers are not used to printing in *standard* lower/case print, a conscious attempt to be consistent is recommended.

Since there are *no* high, middle low discrimination factors involved in the standard upper/case letters, these letters must be identified by placing them next to the already known lower/case letters such as:

a *A*   b *B*

They should also be presented two at a time for discrimination purposes.

The letter discrimination patterns will play an important part in developing a sight vocabulary through configuration. The sequence presented in this section was designed for a coordinated approach to visually discriminating letters as they appear in words. As an advanced reader, your major method of word attack revolves around instant recognition of the specific sequence of letters found in a given word. For the beginning reader these patterns must be pointed out and they should be made aware of the unique pattern of many words.

Auditory Discrimination

Auditory discrimination implies that a student might discriminate between various sounds. As with any discrimination, the only way one can hear something and say it is different from something else is through a comparison of two or more items. The comparison must also have a measurement that is used to compare both items. For example, if you heard a lion roar, is his roar loud or soft? It is loud if you compare it to a kitten but it is soft if you compare it to the roar of the water going over Niagara Falls. As with the visual discrimination, the first step in preparing a student to discriminate sounds should be the difference between large areas of sound. Many people can tell you that music is being played but not what instruments are playing the melody or the tune. It is only with training that independent sounds are separated and identified. The world about us is filled with all types of sounds and they remain at the noise level until they are separated.

The first presentation should be a series of random noises, possibly collected on a portable recorder, and the students should be asked to separate the various noises into groups. You might have different, common, animal noises, common machine noises, and various human speech noises collected on your tape.

Have the students find a picture that might show what made the noise on the tape. Pictures of cars, instruments, people, cats, drills, water, cranes, boys, girls, wind, baby, bell, police car, etc., could all be classified under four sources of noise.

Sounds

human   machine   animal-nature

The conclusion that you should lead the students to understand is that sounds are made by four major sources and they should be able to recognize the major source of each independent sound.

The second stage in auditory discrimination is with the use of words. Short words versus long words. The major portion of the basic communication vocabulary, 70%, is made up of one syllable words. A long word would be one with two or more syllables. Have the students listen to a series of words such as:

Long Words	*Short Words*
window	sky
butterfly	sit
automobile	us
chicken	me
brother	go

They should be made aware of the difference between a long word and a short word. Bring to their attention that when saying a long word you open and close your mouth or move your lower jaw (chin) two or more times. With a short word you only make one down-up motion with your mouth. Have the students place their hand under their chins lightly (not holding it closed or resting on it) and repeat after you several long and short words.

Ask them how many times the mouth opened and closed when they say a word like *breakfast*. The chin will move down and up two times. Then give them a short word like *run*. The chin will go down and up only once.

At this point the movement of the mouth when saying different words should be connected to the concept of syllables. Each time your mouth moves down and up in a word will tell the number of syllables there are in the word. *Elephant* has three syllables; *because* has two syllables; *but* has one syllable. When the student answers, be sure he repeats the word *syllable* or *syllables*. Because of different pronunciations, the student might not repeat all the syllables found in a given word. The teacher should listen carefully to a student's pronunciation if he, the student, comes forth with a different number of syllables in a word. These should be accepted if it is the standard pronunciation the student normally uses in everyday language. The students should be able to quickly identify the number of syllables in long words and short words (one) before moving to the auditory discrimination of vowels and consonants.

Step three involves the basic difference betweeen a vowel and a consonant. A vowel is made with the mouth open and the air from the mouth is unobstructed. A, e, i, o, u are the vowel letters used to represent speech sounds as probably most students will be able to tell you. The consonants are all other letter sounds. They are made with two types of obstructions. The first is a plosive. B, p, k are examples of a puff of air being let out of the mouth like a small explosion. The other type of consonant is called a fricative. This consonant is made by causing the air to vibrate, or given some friction like pulling a piece of wood over some sandpaper. F, s, v are examples of a fricative.

The visual difference between a vowel and a consonant is the open or closed position of the mouth. Have the students observe your mouth in its *initial* position when you give them a word and ask them to tell you whether the word begins with a vowel or a consonant. Examples might be:

apron	—	bug
ice	—	possum
eat	—	father
only	—	vegetable
use	—	manager

Have them repeat the various words after you and notice the position of their own lips, teeth or tongue when they begin the given word. They should also notice the student next to them, as well as the instructor's mouth position. Remember, there must be a contrast for discrimination to take place so as you introduce each of the consonant or vowel sounds in the initial position it should be in pairs. An example might be:

"Here are some words in which we use the alphabet letter 'b' when we write these words. Listen to the words, watch my mouth position at the beginning of each word. Remember, it begins with the consonant 'b'."

> beads
> bread
> boy
> body
> bake
> buddy

Have the students repeat the word after you. Ask them to provide further words that start with the consonant sound "b."

The *same lesson* should include a vowel sound represented by an alphabet letter such as:

> enough
> each
> eat
> eagle

You may present two different consonants or a vowel and a consonant during one lesson but be sure there is something to contrast one sound against another sound available so the student can discriminate.

After each three sets (six sounds) have been presented you should review by giving three or four words and asking for the one different word among the other words given.

Step four would be using and identifying the vowel or consonant sound in different positions, the middle, end, or two or more different sounds found in one word.

A note of caution as to the spelling of words, silent letters or sounds, and spellings of c, q, r. People agree in our society that we might use "hello" as a greeting or "goodby" as a parting remark. We do the same many times in spelling such as, phone, eye, cat, quick, or house. We agree upon a spelling pattern. The poor relationship between sounds and symbols must be recognized in each word as it appears as an independent item. Some phonic generalizations have been reviewed by Aaron [9] and might prove helpful to both teachers and student.

---

[9] Ira Aaron. *Teaching Word Recognition Skills*. Atlanta, Georgia: Georgia State Department of Education, 1970, pp. 31–58.

Auditory discrimination of sounds should proceed from a recognition and discrimination of noise, to words and syllables, to vowel and consonant sounds as represented in words by the alphabet letters. The initial, final, and medial positions of sounds should be taught so that all the words can be pronounced and used as a word attack skill. Sounding out a printed word has as its prime objective the possible recognition of the word when heard through its oral pronounciation. The reader might have a basic reference to the unknown printed symbols through his oral vocabulary.

Writing Visual-Motor Coordination

In order to avoid unnecessary confusion between reading and printing the common letter formations used in most printed materials it is recommended that all writing (printing) be done with standard print. The need for clear, understandable writing in the business world has been reported for many years. Each year over a billion dollars is lost because of illegible writing. The Post Office Department has millions of letters each year winding up in the dead letter office mainly because of illegible handwriting. For many years cursive writing has caused the young children in our schools untold misery when they are switched from manuscript to cursive writing in about the second grade. The justification of this switch to cursive writing has been fluency, accuracy, and individuality. As to fluency, or speed, a good manuscript writer can keep up or surpass any cursive writer; the accuracy certainly has been disproven throughout the business world for years. The only item that seems to come through is individuality, so much so, that only the individual can read his own writing. It's gotten so that you don't even have to sign your own paycheck, but rather it's deposited for you by the company in the bank. Your Social Security number seems to be the single most important individual identification available today.

Manuscript printing of the standard lower/case letters should be started when you introduce the first set of visual letter discrimination patterns. The basic strokes involve straight and curved lines. If the readiness program has been successful, then the directions for forming the letters in terms of position or volume will be identified by the learner.

For many years the teaching of manuscript writing has used three lines. You should study carefully the presentation of the use of five lines for the initial teaching of the alphabet letters. If you cover the bottom, or top half of the standard lower/case alphabet it becomes clear that the median, or middle line controls the entire alphabet. For example:

Median — — a e k

You will notice that the median line controls where the center line in a given letter will appear. For purposes of clearly viewing the high, middle, and low letters this type of five lines should be placed all across the board.

The top and bottom line should be made with white chalk, the middle dashed line could be made with a red or pink chalk, the other color chalk so it would look like this:

```
_____white
_____blue
— — — — — — — — — — — — — — — — — — — —red
_____blue
_____white
```

There should be a little more space between the blue and the white lines. This was designed so that the high and the low letters will be slightly exaggerated for visual discrimination purposes. If you can find a music scale marker, you can use the three center holders for the blue and red chalk lines and then place the white lines about 2 inches wider on the top and bottom.

The first step in teaching the manuscript writing is to identify the lines. "The top line is white, all high letters will start here. The bottom line is white, all low letters will end here. Point to the top blue line, the bottom blue line, all middle letters will touch these two lines. Point to the middle line. It is red. All of the letters will use this middle line."

It is important that the students discriminate between top-bottom, top blue line, and bottom blue line.

Step two would be to proceed with the same letters you have used to develop visual discrimination. Make sure they can visually discriminate the two different letters *before* they learn to write them. An example using "b" and "p" might be as follows:

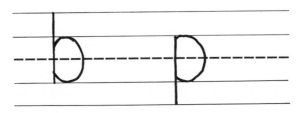

The letters "a" and "d" would be as follows:

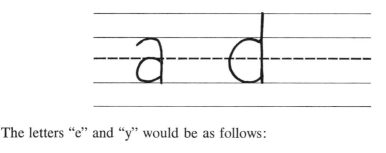

The letters "e" and "y" would be as follows:

When you, as the instructor, do any printing on the board make sure you use the proper print. Each pair of letters presented in the visual discrimination section should be introduced as a writing lesson as soon as possible. As soon as eight or ten letters have been mastered some short words may be presented for practice. Each section should complement the other in the development of unlocking the printed code used in reading. The instructors should keep in mind that this preparation is for a lifetime of use and it involves the key to almost a half million words. Mastery should be strived for *before* the next step is presented. Do not try to cram in as much as possible in one session, but rather build a solid foundation of understanding with each student. It is strongly recommended that once the student has mastered manuscript writing you *do not* try to change him to cursive writing. If you wish to teach him how to sign his name you can do so but all other writing *should remain* in clear, accurate, manuscript writing.

Word Recognition Skills

Understanding the meaning of a word requires that the reader must have some basic reference to the communication. It might be a direct experience, or one that is connected to another type of experience used for comparison. For example, "Her hair was as soft as silk." "He was like a mad dog." The general terms used to indicate an independent method of unlocking the meaning of a printed word are 1) sight words (configuration), 2) phonetic analysis, 3) syntax (word structure), 4) context, and 5) dictionary.

Sight words are identified through the recognition of the shape and sequence of letters which have been stored in the memory. When a letter combination appears in print it is matched to the stored unit and the word is identified. Beginning students have problems identifying those words which do not have outstanding different characteristics, for instance, was, were, or the similar patterns of where and when. The reversal patterns of *on* for *no,* or *was* for *saw,* or *tub* for *but* are the result of not viewing the left to right pattern found in English. This pattern of left to right *must be learned.* Mistakes of reversals do not indicate brain malfunction as many authors suggest, but rather a training problem that can be, and most often is, corrected. When assisting the students in developing a sight vocabulary have them point to the sequence of letters, note the high, middle, low letters and some varied meanings the word might have when used in different sentences.

Phonics deals with the relationships of sounds to the alphabet symbols. The prime purpose of sounding out words is to tap the listening vocabulary. The oral stored memory units far exceed the visual reading units of words for adults requesting training. (This is true of children also.) The initial consonant or vowel is the most important clue used in sounding out words. The practice given in the Auditory Discrimination section of this guide, if complete, will greatly improve the use of this word attack skill as a means of unlocking unknown words through the oral stimulus.

Syntax or word structure can be used in its simplest forms to assist the students in unlocking an unknown word. It should be brought to the student's attention that certain combinations of letters, or independent letters, add additional means to words. Introduce prefixes such as:

un	—	not
in	—	not — or into
re	—	back, again
sub	—	under
dis	—	from, apart
dis	—	not
com	—	with
pre	—	before

Compound words, two or more words making up a single word, such as baseball, railroad, or newspaper can be observed by the students. Suffixes such as *ly, or, er,* which are commonly used in the oral language should be identified. Plurals, s or es, when added to words, denote more than one. The oral language pattern will assist in these distinctions, the transfer is to make the student aware of it in the printed form.

A more complex study of words can be developed later through the basic root words found throughout the language such as: malfunction, malpractice, malignant, malice, using the basic meaning of *bad*. The use of basic roots should be kept in its simplest forms: dark, darker, darkest.

Contextual clues are used by identifying the known words, both before and after, that surround the unknown word. A student should be taught to use the entire selection: the paragraph, the sentence, and the words in the sentence, to assist him in identifying the unknown word. If he cannot recall the configuration pattern, sounding it out fails, trying prefix root, and suffix identification does not help to unlock the word, contextual clues should be attempted. This skill is activated by selecting the known word and assessing its association to a possible meaning of the unknown word. For example:

The dam broke and the town was *inundated*. The unknown word *inundated* might be obtained by selecting the words that precede it.

What might happen if the dam broke?

Answer: The water would come out. It would cause a flood.

Now look again at the sentence and our unknown word. What do you think it might mean?

answer: flooded
inundated = flooded

The general sentences and paragraphs that follow would most likely reinforce the basic assumption of the unknown words. The students should be taught to go beyond the unknown word for further checks.

The process is taking the known memory responses and unlocking the unknown through association and by using a logical conclusion based upon the facts presented.

A further check, but a poor one in terms of excessive use, would be the dictionary. The dictionary depends on two major items: sequence, and association.

Sequence in terms of the progression of a to z. It presupposes a general knowledge of the possible spelling patterns or at least the initial syllable. The first, second, or even the third order progression of alphabetizing should be done in rapid succession so that the use of the dictionary, in terms of its mechanics, is completed in a *short* period of time (not the present two or three year period used in most school texts).

The second major item is association of other alternate names for a single item. The need to have the student use many synonyms, for a given item, will help him in both the dictionary retrieval and other sources of information such as the almanac, yellow pages, catalogues, or any index using various names for the same item. For example:

1) wood, lumber, building products, millwork
2) automobile, car, transportation, auto
3) saw, tools, power tools, hand tools, machines

All of these word-recognition tools depend upon the use of the known stored stimulus to unlock the unknown meaning of a word. The student matches the incoming stimulus with a stored unit and in terms of its relationship of one to another, produces an answer. All of these word-attack skills are procesesd through the intellect.

Written Symbolic Code—Mathematics

Mathematics involves a symbolic code and uses lines to represent a volume referent. The way the positional references are used is similar to the reading code. This is a high number, this is a low number, this is over, this number is under and so forth. If you ask a hundred people to write the first ten numbers you would have almost the entire group write 1 2 3 4 5 6 7 8 9 10. This is a basic problem when trying to introduce the prime concepts in mathematics. The *correct* response to that question, "Write the first ten numbers" is, 0 1 2 3 4 5 6 7 8 9. It's so important that whole disciplines in mathematics function between the 0 and 1, such as algebra, geometry, trigonometry, fractions, decimals, basic and advanced statistics. They all depend on a clear concept of the 0. If you were to give two people something (candy or a drink), and give the third person none, he would certainly tell you in no uncertain terms that he has *none*. Zero is a synonym for none, nothing, or never. This is a basic concept even a three-year-old can demonstrate, no less an adult learner.

The shape of each of the numbers should be taught in pairs, and by using manipulatory objects, the concepts of zero, one, two, etc. should be developed. They should also be introduced in pairs for discrimination purposes. The second step to be learned is the basic grouping of numbers and objects in terms of odd and even numbers.

Whenever the numbers are written in sequence they should always begin with the zero.

0 1 2 3 4 5 6 7 8 9

even   *odd*

0 2 4 6 8   1 3 5 7 9

The volume references listed in Appendix A should be viewed with the basic numbers.

When the basic signs of mathematics are taught, in pairs only, the zero should always be referred to.

0 1 2 3 4 5 6 7 8 9

>	away from zero
<	back towards zero
+	away from zero
—	back towards zero
×	away from zero
÷	back towards zero

The basic meanings involved with each term, add, subtract, etc. should be explained in terms of the sign and the word.

+	add, plus, and
—	subtract, minus, from
×	multiply, times
÷	divide, into
>	greater than, more than you have
<	less than, lower than you have

Each student should also be taught to recognize the written word symbol for each numeral one, two, three, etc.

Basic arithmetic should be a part of any literacy program. One of the best methods to do mathematical figuring and problems is with money. Have the students demonstrate their ability to make change, read numbers in newspaper ads; which cost more, which cost less, and so on.

The practical aspect of showing how to assess how they may get more for their money by understanding how many ounces there are in a pound, by reading and comparing package labels and cost, will greatly assist them with today's sophisticated packaging.

The mathematics to be taught in adult classes must have a meaning to their everyday living, as should all training, and can be a major means of the students' observing quick results from their decision to return to school. When you affect the pocketbook you have hit a major spot for the economically deprived. It can be done by providing a base reference in reading and by having them work with numbers, using the things in the world about them: food, clothing, and shelter.

COMPREHENSION

Operations of the Intellect

The following intellect model is presented in order to clearly understand the various steps in developing and teaching of comprehension involving written materials.

Intellect Model

operation:

Convergent or Divergent Production (external)

Memory
Cognition

Units
   Relations
      class
      system

Products
(Internal)

Stimulus Content throughout the senses:

sight
sound $>$ symbolic

taste
touch $>$ matter as $\Leftarrow$ solids / liquids / gas
smell

Operation of the Intellect

Cognition is the input stimulus which can be consciously or unconsciously presented to the intellect for processing. For example, you might have a band playing music without recognizing the individual instruments. You might see a mountain but not observe the folds in the earth.

Memory is the storage units that have been presented through the senses and processed in some form through the intellect. These are the units that will be used to compare future input units.

Convergent Production is when an individual performs some overt, external act, based upon an observable set of input stimuli. For example, if you act out the movements of making a telephone call and the person observing your actions has seen or used a telephone, he will say, "You are making a telephone call." His answer is based upon your actions; he has put together the several acts and compared them with stored memory acts and used the data to produce his answer. Likewise, if you asked him to tell you what kind of an animal you are talking about he might use the input data to converge on an answer. "He lives in trees, swings by his tail, eats bananas. What is it? It's a ? (monkey)."

Divergent Production can be of two types. The first type is an unstructured divergent production. An example might be a random answer to just fulfill a response request from you. "Joe, how much is two and one?" Answer: "500." He selected any *number* just to give you an answer. He processed the information you gave him, but only insofar as it pertained to numbers.

A *structured* Divergent Production is one in which an individual processes the data input and then uses a further memory unit to produce what has been called the "creative" or unique answer. "John, how much is two and one?" Answer: "If you put them side by side it is 21, if you reverse them it is 12, if you add them it is 3, if you subtract them it is 1. Are they both positive numbers?" He uses the presented structure to deviate from and adds other units to it.

Stimulus Content through the Senses

The only way that the intellect can receive data to be processed is through the senses. The vibrations must be at the threshold of the human senses. If they are below or above the human threshold, instruments such as a microscope or an oscilloscope must be used. The written codes we know as Language, Art, Mathematics or Music are identical in that they are all symbolic codes that use lines to represent some object or item which a group agrees upon as to its meaning. When the senses are activated, the data is processed through the intellect in the identical manner, that is, one input unit against one stored memory unit, no matter what written form the symbols presented have. The product of this relation can either be stored in the memory or acted upon in an external manner by an overt act. For example, a person smells a pot of fresh coffee cooking and thinks it surely would be nice to have a cup of coffee, but does not produce any overt act. On the other hand, he might smell the coffee and say, "How about a cup of coffee?" All data is originally entered through the senses and it is the manipulation of different units within the human intellect that produces new and unique products. Einstein could not have produced his theory without some knowledge of mathematics, etc.

Products (Internal)

Units are the individual items presented to the intellect through the senses. Oral language is used to identify these items in terms of communicating from person to person. If you are going to communicate with another person, the two must agree on a sign to represent a given item or action. "This is the sun; that is water."

Relations are the process of the intellect. It is through the comparison of the input stimulus to a stored memory unit that the item is discriminated in terms of its position or volume. One item can be seen only in its relation to another item. The unit of *measurement* must be the same for the two items. A short piece of string is only short in relation to another piece of string. By itself, it is neither short nor long. A common unit of measurement is its relative length, for instance, in terms of inches (volume).

Classes are groups of things that have some measurement, position, or volume that are the same.

Grow Under Ground	*Grow Above Ground*
carrot	lettuce
potato	corn
radish	spinach
turnip (root)	peas

There are many different ways to classify these items but it will always depend upon your measurement tool which will determine your class. Hard-soft, big-little, one-many, or color might be other ways to classify these items.

A *system* is a broad concept, or category, which would include several classes, yet it will use a measurement factor.

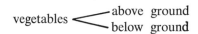

One of the measurements might be that these plants are plants that humans can eat without ill effects.

As all these internal products indicate, they might be stored in the memory without the person displaying an overt act, when the results of the products are converted into an external act, we can observe a convergent production or a divergent production.

Through behavior, such as actions or oral language, we can observe how a human has processed the input stimulus. We can see to what extent he has completed his thinking process. For example, does he process the information through the various relations, steps of classes or systems, or does he repeat the information at the unit level without any further process?

Comprehension of information requires that the information be processed through its relations and then grouped into classes and major systems.

Comprehension of Reading Material

Gagné and Wiegand [10] noted that a significant difference was found in students who were exposed to the use of a topic sentence as an organizer in remembering facts before a retention test. Comprehension was improved through activating those classes and relationships which were attached to the topic in question.

Friedman and Knight [11] state that the "Comprehension is largely a central process, or activity of the brain. . . ." The process is the processing of the data through the intellect by comparing the stored memory units with the basic input stimulus questions. It is the classification of given information into classes and systems in terms of their relations. Generally, the major missing item has been the knowledge of what is used to measure the data. What is the common measuring device through which the information is to be compared? If one item can only be discriminated when another item is given, *both* must be measured by a single instrument. What instrument do we use in history, mathematics, English, art, geography, or economics? As was shown with the classes of vegetables, there can be many ways of classifying them: above ground-below ground, hard-soft, big-little, green-yellow, and so on. Many of today's classes require the student to memorize and return the facts without processing the information any further than the unit level. Nor do the teachers assist the students in classifying the data into basic groups according to a given measurement. Yet, the teachers insist upon the main idea of the data from the students which indicates they want the system production without either having classes or relations developed. The following examples are sample lessons which assist the student through the entire scale of intellectual products:

Intellect "Product" Scale #1

Units (Names of individual items)
      baseball, checkers, tennis, football, pool (billiards), hockey, cards, soccer

    Relations (positional — volume discrimination)

---

[10] Robert M. Gagné and Virginia K. Wiegand. Effects of a Superordinate Context on Learning and Retention of Facts. *Experimental Publication System,* APA, 1970, 7: p. 245–4.

[11] Lora Friedman and David Knight, *Handbook for Teachers of Reading in Adult Basic Education.* University of Mississippi, 1970, p. 17.

large numbers of players — small numbers of players
participant — spectator
high scoring — low scoring
contact — no contact
short game — long game
winter game — summer game

Classes (groups of similar units)

Indoor	Outdoor
checkers	baseball
pool	tennis
cards	football
	hockey
	soccer

System (includes all classes) — *Games*

Teacher Checks
Whole — Part (Deductive Thinking)

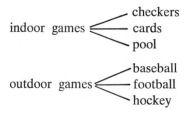

Part — Whole (Inductive Thinking)
What game uses a ball, has nine players, and in which three strikes are out?

Intellect "Product" Scale #2

Units

help wanted, editorial, local news, national news, food ads, world news, department store ad, doctor's column.

Relations

food — clothing
big ad — small ad
big news story — small news story
long article — short article
local — national
first page — last page

Classes

Advertising	News
help wanted	editorial

food ad   local news
department store ad   national news
                           world news
                           Dr. column

System

Newspaper information

Teacher Checks

Whole — Part (Deductive Thinking)

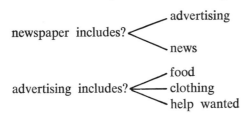

Part—Whole (Inductive Thinking)

What portion of the paper am I reading?
Salesman needed, good pay, must have car.

Intellect "Product" Scale #3

Units

New York, Florida, Maine, Connecticut, North Carolina, South Carolina, Rhode Island, Georgia, Virginia, Delaware, Maryland, New Jersey

Relations

big state — small state
warm state — cool state
high state — low state
long state — short state
manufacturing state — farming state
few people — many people

Classes

Northern States	*Southern States*
New York	Florida
Maine	Virginia
Connecticut	North Carolina
Rhode Island	South Carolina
Delaware	Georgia
Maryland	
New Jersey	

System

East coast of the United States

Teacher Checks

Whole — Part (Deductive Thinking)

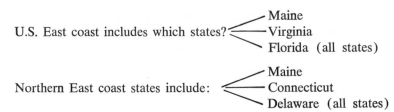

U.S. East coast includes which states? — Maine / Virginia / Florida (all states)

Northern East coast states include: — Maine / Connecticut / Delaware (all states)

Part-Whole (Inductive Thinking)
What state am I talking about?
It is the largest state east of the Mississippi, has its capitol at Atlanta, is called the Peach State, it's a Southern state.

The three "Product" scales are outlines showing the processing of data through the four steps involved in comprehension. Each step is at a different level but the process is identical. It is one stimulus (internal or external) compared with one stored memory unit resulting in a single product. (A to B = C)

The different levels are developed by the different types of comparisons or measurements used by the individual. The training an individual receives in processing information through as many levels as possible will enable him to take other input data and process it through in a like manner. The adult world about him constantly presents input data to be processed by the individual. The prisoner who is asked about the results of his crime, as to whether or not he thought about hurting someone, or being caught, and responded with, "I never thought of that," is probably speaking the whole truth. He has not been taught to think beyond his immediate action. He only processes the information to one level, never making comparisons with alternative units. Comprehension of formal school disciplines, depends upon a) the data input, b) the training received by the student, c) teacher's knowledge of how data is processed by the intellect, d) and a transfer into thinking about the actions of others, or things, in the world about him. This entire process is necessary in order to help the student to understand his own behavior in relation to other human or environmental actions.

If we take the areas involving human behavior, such as stories in a newspaper about people (individuals or groups), a basic measurement tool or comparison might be the actions of the group or individual on a scale.

hostile acts
average-normal behavior (acts)
indifferent-non action

In our society, the rules we agree to are standards the group will function with according to written or unwritten laws. These actions and rules will, and do, vary greatly between cultures, and even within a culture.

Take several stories found in a newspaper and compare the average actions of a member of that society and measure the actions of the people found in the story. Where do they fall on the scale? For example, a holdup in which a murder was committed and a millionaire who has a coming-out party for his daughter which costs him two million dollars. Using the needs of our society as the constant, classify the actions of these two individuals.

We can use many different classifications to investigate the actions of these individual stories but the constant will be, "How does it deviate from average behavior accepted by the group?" Individuals are assessed in the same manner by psychologists.

extravert
average
introvert

If one deviates too far from the average, his actions are frowned upon.

Authors use this type of scale to show the actions of various individuals in different situations. Each time, comparing the actions of a character to a normal (average) reaction, using such classifications as:

man — environment natural/supernatural
man — himself
man — and the society he lives in

Why does he act like he acts under these conditions? Is it normal or average; what influences his actions? What type of classification is the person (in the story) using to justify his acts?

Comprehension then might be viewed as understanding acts of both natural and human behavior in terms of a measurement, above or below normal (average) expectations. When we teach the understanding of different sets of classification, or values, used by different people performing the act itself, we are not teaching agreement but rather, *understanding the acts of other human beings*.

What might be considered the simplest of written material, or oral discussion, can be used to develop an awareness of processing information through the "product" scale!

"Product" Scale

Units	Names, identification of individual items
Relations	Its position, or volume, in relation to another item

Classes   Items grouped together under some similar
             classification

System   A broad category in which all the types of
             matter under consideration might be included
             (the main idea).

A check, using whole-part or part-whole questions can determine whether or not the student has processed the information or uses the memory storage to compare presented units.

In the whole-part, deductive, type questions the teacher supplies the larger unit and asks the student to supply the parts included in the whole unit. For example,

If I asked you to buy some fruit for me, what might you buy? What is included in the concept of fruit?

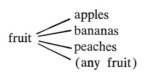

Bring some meat home for supper. What might you bring home?

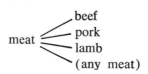

When using the indicative (Part-Whole) type of question, the teacher supplies the smaller units and the student supplies the broader category or item.

"What kind of fruit am I describing?"
"It is long, yellow, you peel it to eat it?" (banana)

"What does this man do for a living?"
"When he gets to work he opens his tool box and takes out his level, ruler, hammer, saw and puts on his nail apron." (carpenter)

Comprehension of written material is using the thinking process to relate the material to a present life-situation.

ORGANIZING AN ADULT GROUP FOR INSTRUCTION

Many reports of adult classes include statements about the high rate of drop-out from these classes. The adult, young or old, who has made the tremendous decision to return to a place that has been less than hospitable to him in the past, is going to rapidly assess the situation as to "the same old thing again," or "I'm certainly glad that I gave it another chance." The wide variety of reasons for coming back to school, the wide range of backgrounds, the vast range of non-readers to poor readers, to one who would like to finish high school, all must be handled quickly and accurately, for as with most of us, *first* impressions will be extremely important. Each student must be interviewed as soon as possible. Within the first and no later than the second session a quick tentative assessment of the purposes, background, and needs of every individual should be completed.

Teachers in the adult program should use the volunteer services available in every state. The Parent-Teacher Association, wives or husbands, fellow teachers, any paraprofessional adult personnel available in the community should be used for this immediate task.

The teacher can provide the helpers with specific instructions. One or two people can write the profile sheet for each student while another assists in some informal testing. The instructor can immediately start assessing the needs of individuals in light of their purposes for coming back to school.

The profile sheet might look like this:

Adult Education Profile

Name _____

Address _____

Telephone _____

Occupation _____ Employed Yes _____ No _____

Age _____

Schooling _____

    Last attended school: Date _____

Reasons for coming to the ABE program

_____

_____

_____

Reading

Non-Reader _____   Word by Word _____

Beginner _____   Intermediate _____

Suggested Starting Group
    Readiness Group
        Positional — Volume References _____
        Visual Discrimination
            Objects _____ Lines _____ Alphabet _____
        Auditory Discrimination
            Noise _____ Syllables _____ Initial V/C _____
        Manuscript Writing

Beginning Reading Group
    Visual Discrimination Words _____
    Auditory Discrimination   Initial-Medial-Endings
    Short sentences and stories (Pupil-Teacher-made)

Intermediate Reading Group
    Comprehension short stories
    Newspaper
    Retrieval of information
        catalogues
        newspaper ads
        telephone books, etc.
    Classifying information (grouping)
    Study Skills
Material needed to achieve purpose for attending program

It might be advantageous to use one of the oral exams to assess the beginning level of your individual students. It takes only a few minutes to administer to each student and he can at least start in a program. The Gray Oral, Gilmore Oral, or the Spache Oral could be used for this purpose.

Before the group starts, the basic material for each level of instruction should be prepared by the teacher. Facilities to run stencils or ditto masters should be available during the evening hours when most of these classes are taking place.

If you find a group that is advanced and coming, for instance, for the GED program, you will need an additional group.

The entire class can benefit from "whole class" instruction in the presentation of a general skill (Syllables, etc.), but the bulk of the work should be mainly on an individual basis with the teacher as a guide to the next step in a student's training.

Small group instructions and individual work should be assigned each day. Simple home assignments, if the class meets twice a week, will assist in continuous training and the skill-using [12] process.

Possible Materials for Adults

If a person comes to the program with the expressed purpose of passing a written Driver's exam or filling out an application for employment, these types of materials should play an important part of the curriculum developed for *that* person.

Materials specifically identified with little children should be avoided. General reading material such as store catalogues, newspapers, magazines, or the telephone book can be used by a teacher as a great asset to a program. The following materials are some which have been used with success in adult programs:

> Adult Readers — Reader's Digest
> Short Booklets (varied topics) — Fearon Pub.
> Reading Labs — Science Research Asso.
> Multi-Media Kits — Bowman Co.
> What Job for Me Series — Webster Div. McGraw-Hill
> Reading Development Kit A — Addison-Wesley

Teacher-pupil-made materials should be used extensively since the individual student will be involved in the development of themes that interest him. The basic concept of developing a person that is capable of processing information through the "product" scale should be a guiding factor when developing teacher-pupil materials.

Physical Testing

The two major senses, the eyes and ears, should be tested as early as possible in the program.

---

[12] Don Parker, *Schooling for Individual Excellence*, Canada, Thomas Nelson & Sons. 1963.

Eyes should not only be tested for acuity (vision) but also for coordination. A short exam on a testing machine like the Keystone Telebonicular (Meadville, Pa.) will screen out large problems which should be referred to the project director for further action. Many outside agencies are ready and willing to help with these problems and all they need is the cooperation of the school.

Hearing can also be tested very simply on an audiometer. The school nurse, local college, or health department might assist in screening the entire group in a few hours.

Another problem that comes up in adult classes, mostly held in the evening, is that many students have completed a full day's work, (teachers also) and are just plain tired. A short break with a soft drink and a sweet might assist in bringing some energy into the blood stream. If the pace, set by the teacher, is too fast, many students will just say it's too demanding and drop out.

Local health officials, nurses' organizations, should be invited to the class for discussion on mental health, nutrition, drug abuse, available health services, and so on. The reading materials presented in these discussions might be used for training in reading skills and comprehension.

Mental Testing

Testing should be going on continuously during the program with the informal assessment of daily progress. If the student has completed the assigned task, he should be brought to the next step as soon as possible.

Before you enter into formalized testing, the objectives of the testing program should be clearly defined. What are we looking for? Will we find it with this test? What do we intend to do with it when we find it? These questions should be answered before the students are subjected to hours of testing. Remember, psychologically these adults have had very poor associations with testing and it might not be advisable to place them in such a formal testing situation most often required by many standardized tests. Some formal tests available are:

1. Bobbs Merrill Company
        Gray Oral Reading Test, 1963

2. California Test Bureau
        Test of Adult Basic Ed., 1967
        Spache Diagnostic Reading Scales, 1963

3. Follett Publishing Company
        Adult Basic Ed. Student Survey, 1967
        Individual Reading Placement Inventory, 1968

4. Harcourt, Brace and Jovanovich
    Adult Basic Learning Exam, 1967
    Gilmore Oral Reading Test, 1951

Measurement and evaluation in adult classes should be centered on the progress of the individual and his ability to transfer his learning into his everyday life situation. Is the program assisting him in reaching his goals and is it reaching the goals of preparing an individual to cope with the world about him in such a way that he becomes a participating member of society? Many times only the teacher and the student can answer these questions; no formal test can supplant one human understanding of another human's progress.

SUMMARY

When a person receives an incoming stimulus it is matched with a stored unit and the results are either stored in the memory or can be observed as an act, such as speech. The process of the intellect is matching one stimulus unit against one memory unit and discriminating the item in terms of either its volume or its position in space or time. The Key to Learning is to prepare the student to observe data as explained through common language meanings.

Reading readiness is not just training for five or six year old children but rather everyone, if they are to learn to read, must have a proper foundation for auditory and visual discrimination of a written code. This foundation is the mastery of positional and volume references in thinking and language. A student's associations should be identical to the intended meaning of the teacher when he or she explains the reading symbols.

When a teacher explains that "this half circle, or line, is in front of the line," such as found in the b, the student must supply the correct missing associations such as "front not back," "half not whole," "circle not square." Therefore his basic thinking patterns, when using the major positional and volume references, must be attuned to automatically responding with discrimination factors. The student should master the eighty-four basic positional and volume references found in Appendix A before entering into the reading of symbols. This training should take place by having the student manipulate items, drawing, practicing, and demonstrating pairs of references such as on-off, front-back, high-middle-low, or none-one, big-small.

Visual discrimination is the ability to see an object, and by using positional and volume references, identify it apart from all other objects (e.g. The letters of the alphabet.)

Auditory discrimination of human speech sounds is the ability to hear sounds of parts of words, whole words, and distinguish them from all other human speech sounds.

Writing, manuscript printing, should be a major program for developing visual-motor coordination. By using the five line approach the base reference of the median line should assist in developing accurate writers, and develop a solid foundation for visual discrimination of letters and numbers. The only cursive writing that should be taught is the individual's signature.

Each student should understand why and how the word recognition skills are used. The five basic word recognition skills are: sight words, because of their shapes, sounding out words to tap the listening vocabulary, prefixes, roots, suffixes for meanings of parts of the word, context clues for identifying known items to unlock the unknown, and the use of the dictionary as an outside source for meaning.

The major concept in mathematics is the zero. In order for understanding to take place the movement away-from and towards the zero is of paramount importance. Practical application of examples is strongly recommended.

Comprehension of bodies of knowledge must be made through the intellectual process of units, relations, classes, and systems. The student should be made aware of the expectations of what people are looking for when they ask for a main idea, or supporting facts. Grouping and classifying information according to similarities and differences is necessary when dealing with all types of information. Being aware of the yardstick, or measurement, being used when trying to observe or explain human behavior is a basic skill necessary for all individuals when trying to understand the culture or society they are dealing with. Is that an average reaction? How is the action being measured? From what source is the measurement being taken? All of these are necessary to develop a thinking person.

Organizing a class for instruction demands that the person receive immediate attention to his present goals and plans formulated for the long range goals of each individual. Physical limitations should be checked at the very beginning of the session and mental testing should be at a minimum with careful analysis of what the results are going to be used for, training or stored away in a vault where no one sees them.

The program presented in this guide is an outline that, when used correctly, develops the use of the intellect in decoding some of the basic written symbols of our language. The adult who has mastered an oral language has demonstrated beyond any doubt that he or she is fully capable of intellectual discrimination. We have only to open up a new dimension of decoding symbols, classifying information, and a new world is theirs forever.

SELECTED BIBLIOGRAPHY

Books

Brooks, Nelson. *Language and Language Learning* (2nd. Ed.). New York: Harcourt, 1964.

Fitzgerald, James A. and Fitzgerald, Patricia. *Teaching Reading and the Language Arts.* Milwaukee: Bruce Publishing Company, 1965.

Friedman, Lora and Knight, David. *Handbook for Teachers of Reading in Adult Basic Education.* Jackson, Mississippi State Department of Education, 1970.

Knight, David and Friedman, Lora. *Readings for Teachers of Reading in Adult Basic Education.* Jackson, Mississippi: Mississippi State Department of Education, 1970.

Lanning, Frank F. and Many, Wesley (Eds.). *Basic Education for the Disadvantaged Adult: Theory and Practice.* Boston: Houghton Mifflin Co., 1966.

Managano, Joseph A. *Strategies for Adult Basic Education.* No. 11 *Perspectives in Reading.* Newark, Delaware: International Reading Association, 1969.

Otto, Wayne and Ford D. *Teaching Adults to Read.* Boston: Houghton Mifflin, 1967.

Parker, Don H. *Schooling for Individual Excellence.* Canada: Thomas Nelson & Son, 1963.

Parker, Don H. *Schooling for What?* New York, N.Y.: McGraw-Hill, 1970.

Readings for the Disadvantaged. (Thomas Horn Ed.). New York, N.Y.: Harcourt, 1970.

Smith, Edwin H. *Literacy Education for Adolescents and Adults.* San Francisco: Boyd and Fraser, 1970.

Smith, Edwin H. *Teaching Adult Basic Reading.* Albany, N.Y.: University of the State of New York. State Education Department. Bureau of Continuing Education & Curriculum Development, 1968.

Ulmer, C. *Teaching the Disadvantaged Adult.* Washington: National Association of Public School Adult Education, 1969.

Other Studies

Aaron, Ira E. *Teaching Word Recognition Skills.* Atlanta, Georgia: Georgia Department of Education, 1970.

Anderson, D. & Niemi, J. *Adult Education and the Disadvantaged Adult.* Syracuse, New York: ERIC Clearinghouse on Adult Education, 1969.

Bickley, A. C., Dinnan, J. A. and Bickley, R. Language Association as a predictor of Performance on an Intelligence test. *Journal of Reading Behavior,* 1970, Vol. 2, 291–294.

Brown, D. and Newman, A. Research in Adult Literacy. *Journal of Reading Behavior.* Milwaukee: National Reading Conference, 1970, Vol. 2:1.

Dinnan, James A. The Key to Learning. *Journal of Reading Behavior.* Milwaukee: National Reading Conference, Winter 1971, Vol. 3:1.

Gagné, Robert, Wiegand, V. Effects of a Superordinate Context on Learning and Retention of Facts. *Experimental Publication System.* APA 1970, 7: 245–4.

"Illiteracy in America." *Harvard Educational Review.* (R. Reordanard, W. Smethurst, Eds.) 1970, Vol. 40:2.

Robinson, Richard. An Investigation into the use of the Cloze Procedure with a Group of Functionally Illiterate Adults. Unpublished doctoral dissertation, University of Georgia, Athens, Ga.

Summer, E. G. Material for Adult Basic Education. *Journal of Reading.* 1967, Vol. 10, 457–67.

Journal Sources (Adult Literacy)

National Reading Conference Yearbooks
Journal of Learning Disabilities
Journal of Reading
Journal of Reading Behavior
The Journal of Correctional Education
Adult Education
Adult Leadership

Information Sources (Adult Programs)

American Library Association, Chicago, Ill.

ERIC Clearinghouse for Adult Education. Syracuse, N.Y.: Syracuse University

International Reading Association, Newark, Delaware

National Association of Public School Adult Educators. N.E.A., Washington, D.C.

The National Multimedia Center for Adult Basic Education Administered by: Adult Continuing Education Center
        Montclair State College
        Upper Montclair, N.J. 07043

Publishers, Adult Literacy Materials

Allied Education Council. 630 5th Ave., New York, N.Y. 10020

Behavioral Research Labs. Box 577, Palo Alto, Calif. 94302

Bowman. 622 Rodier, Glendale, Calif.

Fearon Pub. 2165 Park Blvd., Palo Alto, Calif. 94306

Follett Publishing Co. 680 Forest Rd., N.E. Atlanta, Ga. 30312

Gov. Printing Office, c/o Superintendent of Documents, Washington, D. C. 20402

McGraw-Hill Pub. Co., Webster Div. 680 Forest Ave. N.E., Atlanta, Ga. 30312

Prentice-Hall, Inc., Englewood Cliffs, N.J. 07632

Reader's Digest Services. Education Division, Pleasantville, N.Y. 10570

Science Research Association. 259 E. Erie St., Chicago, Ill. 60611

Scott, Foresman Co. 433 E. Erie St., Chicago, Ill. 60611

Steck-Vaughn Co., P. O. Box 2029, Austin, Texas 79767

APPENDIX A

All of these eighty-four basic references should be taught and *demon-strated* by the student in pairs. (high-low) When most of the position or volume references have been mastered and become an automatic response on the part of the learner, the student may proceed with instruction designed to enter the new written code.

Positional References

before — after
front — back
start — end
first — last
left — right

up — down
over — under
top — bottom
high — low
above — below

away — beside
near — far
on — off
apart — together
at — upon

in — out
inside — outside

46

middle — edge
open   — closed
round   — square
curved — straight

Volume References

0 1 2 3 4 5 6 7 8 9
zero   — none, nothing, empty, never
one   — each, alone, only, piece, once
two   — both
3–9   — three, four, five, six, seven, eight, nine
big   — little
all   — some
large — small
short — long
few   — many
full   — empty
all   — none
piece — whole
every — never
half   — whole
lots   — tiny

APPENDIX B

Oral Language Exam

This exam should be given after a substantial amount of training has been given in the use of positional and volume references. You are checking to see if the prime response to a given word is in terms of a contrast. The exam is administered orally to the student, one at a time, in a place where other students cannot listen to the responses. The examiner should write down the response and check it for general patterns of contrast.

Oral Language Exam A

Directions: Give me the first word you think of when I say these words. (Do not give the subject *any* samples.) No time limit. The examiner should write the subject's response on a separate piece of paper.

1. hot	_____	11. in	_____
2. front	_____	12. under	_____
3. top	_____	13. high	_____
4. on	_____	14. inside	_____
5. open	_____	15. old	_____
6. big	_____	16. first	_____
7. full	_____	17. long	_____
8. piece	_____	18. far	_____
9. earth	_____	19. tall	_____
10. straight	_____	20. up	_____

Correct results according to contrast (hot-cold, up-down)
Scoring: Excellent 16–20
Good 12–15
Fair 10–11
Poor 0–9